HEALED BY FEAR

BEYOND THE DUSK OF SHADOWS

AF558945

MEDHA BARTHWAL

Copyright © Medha Barthwal
All Rights Reserved.

ISBN 979-888546465-9

This book has been published with all efforts taken to make the material error-free after the consent of the author. However, the author and the publisher do not assume and hereby disclaim any liability to any party for any loss, damage, or disruption caused by errors or omissions, whether such errors or omissions result from negligence, accident, or any other cause.

While every effort has been made to avoid any mistake or omission, this publication is being sold on the condition and understanding that neither the author nor the publishers or printers would be liable in any manner to any person by reason of any mistake or omission in this publication or for any action taken or omitted to be taken or advice rendered or accepted on the basis of this work. For any defect in printing or binding the publishers will be liable only to replace the defective copy by another copy of this work then available.

This book would not have been possible without the endless dramatics of my brother. Consider this piece of work as a reward for your timeless antics :)

Contents

Contents

Prologue

"I heard the echo for the last time,
and this time I felt its lie,
for I ran after it,
but stopped suddenly,
as a reaisation set it free,
that the echo was me"

Acknowledgements

To, *DJ,* thank you for everything. You will always be the best.

To, Azmena, you are a great motivator and an exceptional paragon. Cherish the roses of the moments for as long as you live.

1. No One Sees It

No one sees it,
the darkness of the mind,
the blinding faith in the eternal star,
the crying river of the soul,
or the dying breath in the hole.

The lost finally found,
the key buried in the ground,
the sadness changed the eyes,
but the path changed the time.

Sorry for the weak,
simple for the drowned,
last for the one,
and killer for the known.

Lying for the freedom,
running for the end,
sleeping in the blissfull pillow,

burning with a friend.

The sound of the empty heart,
the silence of the speaking mind,
the sorrow of the lauging fears,
the happy eye of the gloating tears.
All around the dark knight found,
and the revenge for the unknown,
is helping the sound.

Everyone sees it,
but only what they want,
and the truth of reality,
can never be gone.

See, the fire on the hand,
the killer in the eyes,
the sorrow of the dark,
and the hate in the light,
but how can they,
when everyone is blind?

2. Supernatural

A loud scream in the darkest night,
over the sleeping graves of endless plight.
A sleeping ghost drifting around,
while the ground is crying with a hollowed sound.

A silent laugh, an empty core,
just the devil speaking nothing more.
Living souls never found,
but the dead are laughing all around.

Logic screaming with all its might,
over the deadly beast of imaginative mind.

A damned soul driven mad,
because of the greed of the devil's dad.
A corpse hanging from a tree,
singing a song of loving deed.

Satan dancing on its pentagram,
demons possessing all our souls,
no one stops or all just ignore.

A drop of dark on the soothing soil,
a groove of bones with a bloodshot eye.
The sleeping graves of endless plight,
in the deep silence of supernatural minds.

3. Snowglobe

There in the distance,
a firefly glows,
a drop of dew,
on the petal, it flows.

A silent song slowly whispers,
the sound of the sea echoing around,
and the diamond in the distance,
slowly fades out.

She watches it all,
from her empty broken eyes,
unable to move around,
with her dreams and hopes scattered all around.

Another hope crumbles,
another snowflake falls,
another day of standing still,
and watching her tears grow small.

A shadow flits around her,
as she turns upside down,
unable to hear her own thoughts,
with the pieces of herself,
flying all around.

Only the river calms her down,
with all its flowing stories,
and
letting her listen to its cries,
while her eyes stare at the firefly.

If only the night had turned a little more brighter,
she could have watched that diamond glow,
but for all its worth,
she could finally rest her show.

Surrounded by transparency,
and tired of the falling dome,
with the emptiness weighing her down,
but,
she had given up on her own,

after all,
it was still called her home.

4. Friends

Jumped into the arms of the fallen angel,
when the mind was still young.
Couldn't hold on to it,
but the friends saw through it.

Helped the demons drown,
killed the madness left alone,
travelled through the burning coals,
but still, happiness was shown.

Insanity engulfed the shadows,
tears engulfed the hope,
but, the friends grew the flower,
of darkness's gorgeous powers.

Opened the heart at the crack of dawn,
fought the time under the stars.
Shadows helped lose the guilt felt,
but in the end,

the friends too left.

5. Time

Hoped for the best,
for the glittering thread of the future,
and the forgotten past became the only friend,
but it was just the beginning of the end.

Lost with the mind,
a song that once shined.

The hate full of laughter,
now a bitter light in the sky,
the sweet pillar of shadow,
now a lost soul in the dark.

Sorry found the truth,
giver found the lie,
but in the end,
only the beginning was made to cry.

Smile shut the sorrow,
sorrow ended the tears,
tears fed the fire,
fire healed the wound.

The dark ended want,
for the light's little haunt.

Silence became empty,
freedom hugged the life,
dead became guilty.
So finally,
happiness was the sinner, but deep down,
time was the ultimate winner.

6. Friendly Butterfly

There lies a heart in a wall,
watching the butterfly sing and fall.

The giver took a knife,
and the flower lost its smile.
The ice killed the sound,
and the butterfly fell on the ground.

The demon unleashed its hell,
and everyone surrendered to the glory that befell.

Anger fueled the blood,
and the silence died in the flood.
The butterfly survived the tragedy,
for the beast victimized the flower,
and the cries broke its power.

Four little petals, sleeping in the light,

surpressing an unstable fight,
clinging to the butterfly,
who is finding happiness in the eyes.

Lost is the control,
over the gloomy smile,
but the demon will,
never reach its mile.

A leaf standing its ground ,
while the butterfly is sound asleep,
as the beast fold inwards,
and the flower goes back to its nest.

There lies a heart in a wall,
watching the butterfly sing and fall.

7. Invisible Reflections

I had a face, but no name,
I had a lie, but no truth,
I had a mirror, but no self.

The wall was too high up,
the mirror was too broken,
was I the same person,
whom I remembered?

There was a doom in the eyes of glass,
there was a memory in the brains of past,
but who could gain the face,
if the answer was on the other side?

Just a moment's time,
the anger rushes again,
bringing back the memories of,
this unknown self.

I was in the middle,
not knowing what to say,
the presence behind the mirror,
only chanting one name.

There was a rise of curiousness,
waiting for the light to rush in,
only then I realized,
it was a ruse,
to cover up the darkness.

Forgetting it piece by piece,
I tried to remember the face,
only to make myself,
another shadow of keys.

When both the mirrors disappeared,
only the fading memories were heard,
with two pair of eyes,
gazing into each other's heart,
cause the reflections cracked apart.

8. Ocean of Rain

Hear the faint footwork of the clouds,
it follows the blue of stars,
even if there's a tremor,
trying to keep the sky sane.

Another world stops,
making the light fall,
for the valley below,
is making the sound drop.

A little cry searches,
for the answers hidden in the waves,
but reaches a bloodied path,
and watches itself cave.

Slowly and steadily,
the eyes come to a halt,
still standing under,
the fading dance of the sky,

in the valley of the echoing cry.

Following the fallen drops,
who guide to the lost fears,
even in the thunderous crashing of waves,
and the gloating rain of tears.
When the deed repeats itself,
the night will stop singing,
and the clouds will cease their dancing,
cause everything,
would have lost its meaning.

So, when the sun has set,
and the bloodied path has fallen apart,
in that shadow of pain,
a silver dark will shine,
creating an empty sight,
in the calm ocean of rain.

9. Parallel Thunder

Broken trees, thunderous scars,
climbing the fallen arc,
waiting to see,
if you could do something.

Broken tears, thunderous flowers,
cimbing the hours of dark,
walking the road that was,
torn down for nothing.

One for the crown, two for the home,
wishing for a peaceful throne.
When you know you are a prisoner in every spring,
it will all come back,
no matter where you live.

Standing at the edge,
gazing at the thunder,
wind blowing your hair,

opening up your eyes,
glistening at the sky in wonder.

From the castle above the tower,
an arrow leaves the bow,
going straight at the full blown sky,
trying to harness the lightning's power.

Almost there, touching the throne,
remembering the prison in the spring,
hoping to end it all,
but failing to open the wings.

Just a second of time it takes,
to fall over the edge,
but the sudden appearance of an arrow,
quickly jolts you awake.

The world stops spinning,
watching the game,
if the bow will return to the arrow,
or the lightning will strike again.

The lightning meets the bow,
a spark of pain fulfils it all,
the constant fear of broken tears,
now a healing scar in the dark.

The wings bloom in all their glory,
the throne once again claimed,
it's the thunder of the spark,
helping the crown bear its mark.

All three united in the light,
succeeding each other's night,
the arrow, the lightning and the wings,
making the storm go under,
as they all turn into thunder.

10. Earth's Power

My life is being spun on a bed of barbed wire,
with the light all around,
the black and white leaf,
is spilling ice on the ground.

I was on a boat drifting on the sea,
waves crashing my course,
the shore is near,
but I am too weak with fear.

You will be there sitting on a throne,
when the shadow has deserted its stone,
and the time builts its tower,
then you will see me unleash my mind's power.

Hell ate the greed, and the light got freed,
but it never ended,
because the darkness died in its heat.

Never did the sea,
turn its joy from the open sorrow,
how could it?
cause the ocean sank in the depths of tomorrow.

A dark fire consumed the grey play,
all that was left,
turned into clay.

Life is a grudging past,
silence is the sweet river at the last,
a gold tomb, a silver coffin,
helped the thunder of the near flower,
as I unleashed my mind's power.

11. Snowflower

Waiting for the wind to blow,
to take the world for a ride,
wishing a sweet snow,
on the sloping roofs of pride.

A night it was to remember,
when the laugh was just in reach,
but it all went away,
like a beautiful dream.

Touching the ground softly,
a shadow of snow was born,
what a peaceful time it was,
when no cries were torn.

Like a hopeless mind,
dancing in the light,
unable to let go,
but a snowflake's day,

was all to make it go away.

For long, the ground was silent,
softly enjoying its peace,
even when,
the sun broke its needs.
Walking down the snowflake street,
a shower of dusk turned around the corner,
with its footsteps glittering in the moon.

The wind finally blew,
bringing the laughs from a dream,
carrying the peaceful time,
and making the winter enjoy its bliss,
for,
it was a snowflower's kiss.

12. Satisfaction

Falling in myself,
with no ocean to support it,
losing all the depth,
in the valley of your wealth.

Living in the shadows,
for little or no night,
swallowing up the heavens,
in the eternity of the meadows.

Holding out the hand,
but never reaching the edge of the broken cliff,
taking in the fear of yourself,
do you hear me now?

Waiting for the moon to shine in the river,
watching the ocean disappear in the mirror,
waiting for you to save the killer,
do you hear me now?

Letting a silent thunder run wild,
hoping for the flower to return to the eyes,
giving it all up for myself,
do you hear me now?

It was a scream,
in the seventh hour of blue,
it was a laugh,
in the patience of chaos,
do you hear me now?

Going into the bottomless ocean,
leaving all the broken mirrors,
hiding all the deepest fires,
enjoying all the shattered reflections,
do you see me now?

13. Shadow

I saw a hidden gem,
glowing faintly in the mirror,
but I tried to run from its smiles,
until I felt a shiver.

A wilted flower, stared at me for long,
but later I noticed,
it didn't have a face.

I looked around the flower,
searching for a face,
but when I offered it mine,
I realized that it needed a vase.

The flower was attached to the dark,
which looked at me with contempt,
so I ran away again,
but could feel it following behind.

It followed my every move,
even in the light,
it stayed with me forever,
even when I hit a dead end.

I ignored all its lessons,
I ignored all its cries,
I ignored all its simple laughs,
cause I was too busy holding up my disguise.

No matter where I went,
it reminded me of my hidden gem,
for it sensed my dangers,
even before I could breathe.

So finaly I stopped running,
and acknowledged the defeats,
but I took too long,
cause there were no advice,
to warn me of the dusky song.

I searched for the dark,

far and wide,
trying to make it mine,
and turn back the time.

It found me again,
and stayed as still as possible,
waiting for me to use the gem,
and make it mine.

So finally, I realized the mistakes that I made,
and unveiled the hidden wings,
with a glowing gem portrayed.

I tried soaring upwards,
in the pale moonlight,
and noticed the shadow following,
with its wings spread,
and the wilted flower,
glistening above its head.

14. Hope

When the light will cease to exist,
when the eyes will loose their shine,
when the silence will be loud,
then only the dark will be embraced.

Never did the light shout,
never did the tongue spill its secrets,
never did the laughter find any happiness,
then only the insanity was missed.

Lost the cheery soul,
lost the heart inside,
lost the ordinary night,
Then only the imagination found its cries.

Fought the fire,
proved the weird child,
found the unique desire,
gained all the pain.

The world gave up its silence,
and the light gave up its care,
the hate turned to strength,
and the past ate up its fear.

Took all the experience,
threw away the path,
found a lovely star,
lived in the ice,
and reached a strong chance.

Loved the butterflies with all of the heart,
took the hand of the constant river,
and when all that remained,
was the emptiness,
hope played its part.

15. Forever

All around is a burning fire,
and a sweet sound,
drifting through the caved ocean
and a rustling tree,
watching the sigh of joy,
that leave from your far away gaze,
and a serene look in your eyes.

I saw your better half,
I saw you leave your place ,
I saw you harboring the beasts,
I saw you,
forgetting the face.

Soft as snow,
your broken pieces melt,
and a new spring shines,
and a kind fear,
replaces your grim side.

You welcome me in your soft glow,
and a song slowly fills,
the empty parts of this night,
for you stay with me,
as I show you my,
painful lights.

A rose petal falls,
at the sound of your voice,
as your fingers linger on the petal,
and I feel your heavenly smiles.

Day and day again,
in a fond lie of time,
I feel the string of fates,
intertwining our designs.

This is where it began,
this is where it will end,
cause I will always hold your hand,
and we will be leave here together,
for you engraved my heart in yours,
until the end of forever.

16. Empty

The night sky full of laughs,
drinking the star's cries,
watching the grief down below,
in its empty oceanless eyes.

Would you look at the moon if it didn't give out any light?
Slowly taking in the light around,
waiting for the soul to grow,
even in its deep bright mind,
once lied the empty door.

Will the pain be visible if there were no wounds to heal?
A lie, a betrayal, stole away the warm smile,
leaving a bitter hope of sadness,
drowning in the empty cries.

Would you still be here if the soul had already left?
Walking down the lonely road,
wondering why there were no signs,

taking a look at the past,
thinking if everything was really fine.

Will the ocean shine in its own smile if the sky appeared dark?
Those emotionless flowers,
drawing all the might,
burning in hell,
the empty pain of the night.

What if you could look at the darkness like you look at the light?
All alone, the cloud slowly fades,
leaving a river of grief,
and watching the pain be the constant companion,
along the fire,
remembering only three words,
it doesn't stop.

17. Crystal Garden

In the garden of lonely tears,
A river of calm flows,
Silencing all the screams,
with an angelic glow.

The flowers of fear,
bloomed all around,
But, you never let them,
fall on the ground.

The seed of the sorrow,
Finally found a friend,
Because, you were the only one,
Who realized that it was a hidden gem.

Even when the calm,
Of the river falls,
You would still be there,
To catch us all.

It was your cry of smile,
Which cured everything wrong,
And the broken leaves of the tears,
Were turned into a song.

Finally, everything turned into cherries and roses,
And a new seed of crystal was born,
Cause you were the one,
Who removed all the thorns.

18. Fire

A voice burning in ice,
the loud scream and cries,
the unleashed beast now about to die,
the flame, the eyes, never to be disceet.

Forged in water,
a truthful hand,
sleeping in the pyre,
of the sorry man.

Sunflower and blood,
hand in hnd,
hard to be recognised,
in the hot sand.

The spark of an enigmatic soul,
ignited my dead tears,
but how could they help,
when I killed my selfless fear?

The burning grove,
stoked the scars.
the wind silenced the roar,
and the dark void filled up on its own.

Overnight the light changed hearts,
swallowing the silence,
and letting the hate,
take up its part.

The grief swallowed vengeance,
the night released the trailer,
how did it end?
with the death of the blackmailer.

The flame of the cuts,
searching the thoughts of past,
the coal that turned everything orange,
now dies to watch it turn blue,
for the eyes did their part, and
once again,
the fire ripped us apart.

19. Abyss

It was a fault, that,
no one could forgive,
it was a fear, that,
no one could outlive.

The fall of a night,
was as calm as a feather,
that blows in the wind,
even in the presence of light.

It was a mistake that
everyone cherished,
it was the tranquility of time, that,
everyone had to perish.

Once undone,
the pieces fell apart,
all that was left,
got buried under the stars.

A guilt of memory,
echoed from below,
reminding the flower of sorrow,
to shine from the willow.

The ashes turned to night,
feeding the fire of the standing grief,
with the sweet melody,
of broken ice.

Forget the past,
fight the way,
it could have been satisfied,
if only there was a grave.

Spiraled down the cliff,
with the prospect of an invisible dawn,
trying to forgive the finished deed,
but was too drunk,
in the cries of bliss,
to realize, that,
it was my own fallen abyss.

20. Healed by Fear

Would you smile like the sky?
if no one heard that cry?
for I disguised my eyes in the red,
getting it higher up in the mind,
almost near the edge,
but was that enough to break and let go?

I am giving it up,
there's a scream in the night,
I am letting it up,
there's a dread in the eyes, that you can't find,
I am swallowing it up.

All of it gone in the nick of time,
so I buried it up in front of your eyes.
There's nothing to see,
there's nothing to be,
anymore.

There's a crease on the breeze,
flying far away,
no one sees it but me,
there's a dread in the eyes,
I lost it all behind,
Everything is healed by the fear.

Follow the trail I left,
to see what I see,
since you are the one,
who set it for me.

Dreading all the lies,
they can fire up the pyres,
everything is healed by the fear.

Getting it higher,
all the way up,
ignoring the fiery tears, cause
everything is healed by fear.

21. Still Here

You were standing there,
like a summer of spring,
for I was watching you,
like a shower of rain,
but you,
calmly drifted off to your pain.

Years leave for eternity,
with seven more to go,
cause, a little of your darkness,
kept me afloat.

If only you could answer,
all the lingering questions of your eyes,
then maybe I could have stopped myself,
from ruinig my image of your smiles.

Your voice echoes each day,
from the cliff you once stood,

for I trace myself back,
only to hope for your,
ocean of broken tears.

It was a starry night of eve,
and the moon glowed in your day,
for I wanted to give you an endless night,
but you silently flew away.

Its the fall of grey now,
and your hand still stays in mine,
and my heart still follows your smile,
for,
if I had to forgive the shadows,
I would make the time go slower,
because for you,
I would do it all again,
a million times over.

22. Moonflower

The moon shone on its tears,
Silently shutting out all its light,
Trying to keep its sanity,
But forgetting that it was all a lie.

The flower looked up at the sky,
Wondering about the abyss of its time,
Slowly swaying away from the reality,
Forgetting that it was all a part of its design.

A show, a cry, a source of energy from another star,
Creating an elaborate mask,
And enjoying the pain of smiles,
While paying the price for its cries.

Another sigh escapes the petals,
Making the night shiver,
Silently laughing in the madness,
And crushing all its dreams.

Both left their heart and scars,
Hoping to end their way,
Sinking in the abyss,
And trying to protect their deepest emotions
For they wore every mask in existence,
In the midst of the fallen ocean

Slowly the night,
Assembles the two broken pieces,
Joining their pains and smiles by the hour
Making them leave all their colors,
And creating the masterpiece,
Known as moonflower.

23. Forgotten Autumn

Walking down a path,
that leads to nowhere,
standing in front of a sign,
that goes back to despair.

Sitting down on a bench,
with me,
watching you slowly turn into a mystery.

Was it the golden leaves?
if it could be the orange sea,
was it gonna be hard to stay with me?

A piece of mine left your mark,
and it was all I could do,
to make you stay for the sake of this world,
while leaving the stone unturned.

So, I am changing all the dawns to dusk,
wishing for the fear to last longer,
only waiting for the chance,
to walk on the yellow road,
into my furthest dreams.

A leaf fell on my shoulder,
the red blooming above,
leaving the bench to wonder,
if there ever was a way.

Slowly the wind changes,
the trees rustling the dreams,
even in the absence of,
your broken leaves.

Acceptance was worth the wait,
finally gripping it tight,
the new bench of the fall,
changing it night by night.

Walking another path of yours,
reminiscing each colour of mine,

while sitting on the old,
autumn bench of pine.

24. Echo

There was an echo in the river,
flowing below my feet,
I bent down to touch it,
but it left me in curiosity's heat.

I heard the echo again,
this time in a blood-curdling scream,
but once again,
it left me in its golden dreams.

I waited for the river to show me the lies,
but it ignored the wishes,
and gathered the truth,
just to flung it all ashore,
as I listened to the first echo.

I heard the echo for the last time,
and this time I felt its lie,
for I ran after it but stopped suddenly,

as a realization set it free,

that the echo was me.

25. Undying Winds

There was a diamond ocean in front of me,
but I chose to turn to the fading storm,
was the wind silent, or
the cry too warm?

I need you to hold on,
even if the shore,
is far away,
for the world out there,
is swallowing the grey.

There won't be someone,
to follow the way,
even in the gloomy hour,
of the ocean winds.

I need you to hold on
just so I can feel the pain,
but it would be fair to say,

that we all fade away.

I need you to stay along,
even if the hold is getting weaker,
just so I could turn your tears,
into a soft healer.
Maybe the rope was too weak,
or the wind was too strong,
cause, in the flow of time,
it was all gone.

I need you to hold on,
make me see your hand again,
just so I can feel the worth of me,
before it follows the grey.

I made you stay in the wind,
but broke the fears again,
for I was on the brink of spring,
and calmly slipped away.

26. Serene

All alone on the dancing river,
there is a star,
dead in its deed,
admiring the glory in sight.

Sitting on the edge of the cliff,
staring at the moonrise,
hearing the silence of the night,
and the wind howling in the right.

The glow of the star slowly fading in the dark,
but portraying a smile on its face,
feeling the serene view,
from miles apart.

Watching the cliff get tired painfully,
and the star slowly silencing its own paths,
a smile flitting on your beautiful face,
feeling the serene view,

from miles apart.

You had let your scream,
travel up your hands,
and hit the edge of the cliff,
not knowing that the star,
was just looking at your guilt.

Little while later,
a sudden realization hit,
you had made a shooting star,
disappear at your hands and guilt.

It was the star which had first forgiven your tears,
but you were too busy,
laughing at your own fears.

In the last moments of each other,
its last breath and your fallin' cliff,
both of you glistened in each other's eyes, wondering,
what a serene view,
from miles apart.

The world is a black and white leaf.

9 798885 464659

Printed by Libri Plureos GmbH in Hamburg,
Germany